W9-APB-923

DRUG AND ALCOHOL DEPENDENCE

Impaired Control • Social Impairment • Risky Use

H. W. Poole

www.av2books.com

MEDIA ENHANCED BOOKS
AV²
BY WEIGL™
ADDED VALUE • AUDIO VISUAL

AV² provides enriched content that supplements and complements this book. Weigl's AV² books strive to create inspired learning and engage young minds in a total learning experience.

Your AV² Media Enhanced books come alive with...

Audio
Listen to sections of the book read aloud.

Key Words
Study vocabulary, and complete a matching word activity.

Video
Watch informative video clips.

Quizzes
Test your knowledge.

Go to **www.av2books.com**, and enter this book's unique code.

Embedded Weblinks
Gain additional information for research.

Slide Show
View images and captions, and prepare a presentation.

BOOK CODE

AVQ88545

AV² by Weigl brings you media enhanced books that support active learning.

Try This!
Complete activities and hands-on experiments.

... and much, much more!

Published by AV² by Weigl
350 5th Avenue, 59th Floor
New York, NY 10118
Website: www.av2books.com

Library of Congress Control Number: 2018941338

ISBN 978-1-4896-7925-3 (hardcover)
ISBN 978-1-4896-7926-0 (softcover)
ISBN 978-1-4896-7927-7 (multi-user eBook)

Printed in Brainerd, Minnesota, United States
1 2 3 4 5 6 7 8 9 0   22 21 20 19 18

072018
120817

Project Coordinator: Heather Kissock Designer: Ana María Vidal

First published by Mason Crest in 2016.

Contents

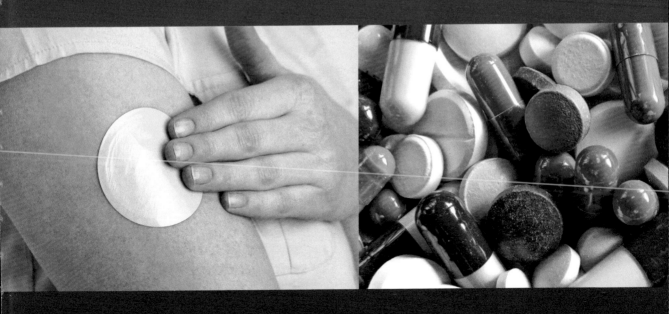

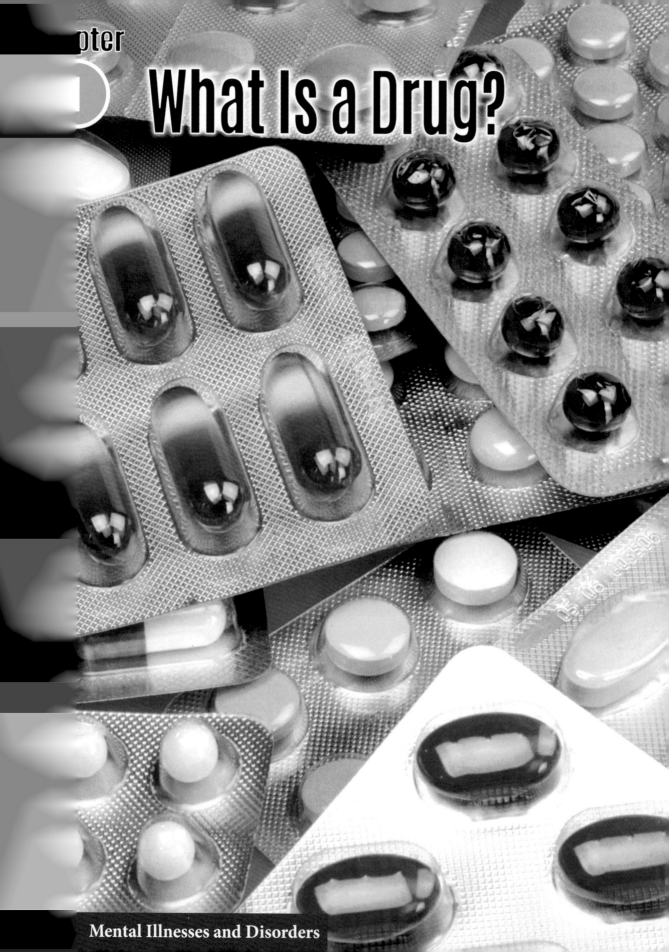

What Is a Drug?

If someone has a health problem, a doctor might suggest he or she take pills that will make that person feel better. Some adults say that they cannot function before they have had their morning coffee. Many adults would also say that a barbecue just is not a barbecue without hamburgers, hot dogs, and a cold beer.

Medicine, the caffeine in coffee and other drinks, and alcohol all have something in common. They are all types of drugs that affect people's brains, bodies, and behavior when they eat, drink, smoke, breathe, or inject them. Not all drugs are bad. Medicine that is prescribed by a doctor can make people healthier or even save their life. Some drugs are harmless in small quantities. When used too much, though, or when used by the wrong person, any drug can have negative consequences, including problems with **addiction**.

Caffeine can make a person feel more awake and alert after taking it.

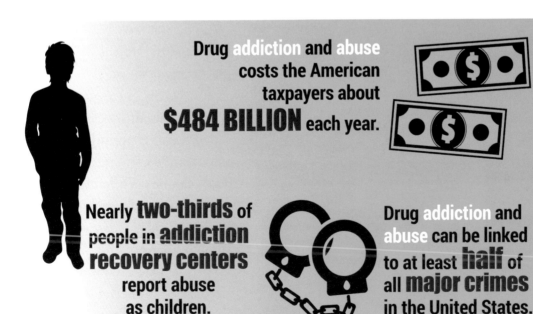

Drug addiction and abuse costs the American taxpayers about **$484 BILLION** each year.

Nearly **two-thirds** of people in **addiction recovery centers** report abuse as children.

Drug addiction and abuse can be linked to at least **half** of all **major crimes** in the United States.

Different types of drugs have different effects on the human body. Some, like caffeine, have such minor effects that people barely think of them as drugs at all. Others are so deadly that the government has made them illegal. Drugs are a huge topic, but there are certain drugs that people are most likely to encounter in daily life.

Medicines

There are a large number of medicines that people take for different physical and mental problems. Some are called over-the-counter drugs because any adult can buy them in a store. For example, people might take an over-the-counter drug such as aspirin to treat a headache. Others are called prescription drugs because people can only get them with permission from a doctor. For example, a doctor might prescribe a drug such as Imitrex for very bad headaches.

Sometimes people buy or steal other people's prescription drugs. One often-abused class of drugs is **opioids**. These are **depressants** that are used for their painkilling effects. Morphine, codeine, and oxycodone are all opioids. Doctors prescribe them to people with serious pain. They are frequently abused by people who do not have real medical needs, though. Heroin is also an opioid, but it is illegal and has no medical use.

Doctors advise against taking someone else's medicine. If the prescription was written for someone bigger, the drug could be too strong. It could cause sickness, coma, or even death. There is also the serious possibility of addiction.

Like opioids, drugs called **sedatives** and **hypnotics** have important uses in medicine. They can be very helpful to people with real **psychological** problems. Also like opioids, though, they are often abused by people who do not really need them. Sometimes even people who need them can begin to take too much. That can lead to problems with addiction.

ALCOHOL USE BY COUNTRY

The World Health Organization (WHO) global report about alcohol usage, published in 2014, contains information about alcohol consumption per year in different countries around the world. Countries listed with very low alcohol consumption have majority Muslim populations. Muslim law, Sharia, forbids the drinking of alcohol, but not everyone obeys that law.

CONSUMPTION PER PERSON PER YEAR COUNTRY	IN LITERS	BEER %	WINE %	SPIRITS %	OTHER %
Belarus	17.6	17	5	47	31
Russia	15.1	38	11	51	0
France	12.2	19	56	23	2
Australia	12.2	44	37	13	7
Germany	11.8	54	27	19	0
Canada	10.2	51	22	27	0
Argentina	9.3	41	48	5	6
United States	9.2	50	17	33	0
Italy	6.7	23	66	11	0
China	6.7	28	3	69	0
Jamaica	4.9	42	5	51	2
United Arab Emirates	4.3	10	3	87	0
India	4.3	7	0	93	0
Ethiopia	4.2	50	1	8	41
Saudi Arabia	0.2	0	2	98	0

Caffeine

This substance is found in coffee, tea, chocolate, and many soda drinks. Energy drinks also have a lot of caffeine in them. Caffeine's **stimulant** effects are not that strong or long-lasting. However, taking in large amounts of caffeine over a short time, or many times over a longer period, can make people sick. Caffeine can also interfere with appetite and sleep. Too much caffeine can cause confusion, headaches, and rapid heartbeat. Withdrawing from caffeine can also cause headaches and muscle aches.

For most adults, drinking alcohol occasionally causes no harm. Drinking too much and too often can be dangerous, though.

Alcohol

Wine, beer, and cocktails all contain ethyl alcohol, which is a depressant. Although people may seem more "up" after drinking alcohol, things are slowing down inside their bodies. When used by adults in **moderation**, and, importantly, when not driving, alcohol is not highly dangerous. If too much alcohol is consumed too quickly, which is called "binge drinking," alcohol poisoning can result. **Seizures**, choking, and **asphyxiation** are just a few of the possible effects. If used in large quantities over a long period of time, alcohol can contribute to organ damage, heart disease, and some types of cancer. Alcohol abuse is the third most common cause of preventable death in the United States.

Sniffing

There are lots of ways that drugs can be taken into the body. People drink coffee and alcohol, and they smoke cigarettes and cannabis. Another way people, especially teenagers, take drugs into the body is by inhaling. It may seem strange that simply sniffing something could qualify as "doing drugs." The chemicals in glue, gasoline, and other substances travel through the nose and eventually reach the brain. Some of these chemicals are extremely powerful. Inhalants are also among the most dangerous drugs. Some can kill instantly, while others can cause permanent brain damage. According to the National Institute on Drug Abuse, the largest at-risk group for inhalant use are adolescents aged 12 to 15.

Ethyl alcohol also affects the mind. It interferes with people's ability to make good decisions. This can lead to many risky behaviors, such as drunk driving, that can end in injury or death. Alcohol is responsible for about 88,000 deaths per year in the United States, including more than 4,000 deaths of people under age 21.

Cannabis

This is the drug in marijuana, which is also called "pot," "grass," or "weed." Like alcohol, it is considered to be a depressant. Marijuana is often smoked, but it can be taken as a pill or mixed into food. Some people use marijuana for medical reasons. It has been found to be helpful to people with cancer, multiple sclerosis, glaucoma, and conditions causing long-term pain. Other people use marijuana because it can bring a feeling of relaxation. However, marijuana can have a bad effect on the lungs and heart, especially when used over long periods. Doctors especially worry about marijuana use in young people, whose brains are still developing. They fear that long-term marijuana use can result in permanent problems with thinking and memory.

One study in New Zealand found that teens who smoked marijuana heavily went on to lose an average of eight IQ points in adulthood.

Nicotine

This is the addictive ingredient in cigarettes, which are made from tobacco plants. Cigarette companies add many other chemicals to them. The many health problems caused by cigarettes include various cancers and very serious heart problems. Chewing tobacco also has serious health risks. Young people who smoke are 10 times more likely to take illegal drugs than those who do not smoke. Unfortunately, nicotine is also one of the most addictive of all drugs. Unlike caffeine, there is no "good" or "safe" amount of cigarettes. The only safe approach to smoking is to never start.

Chapter 2

Drugs and Alcohol in Society

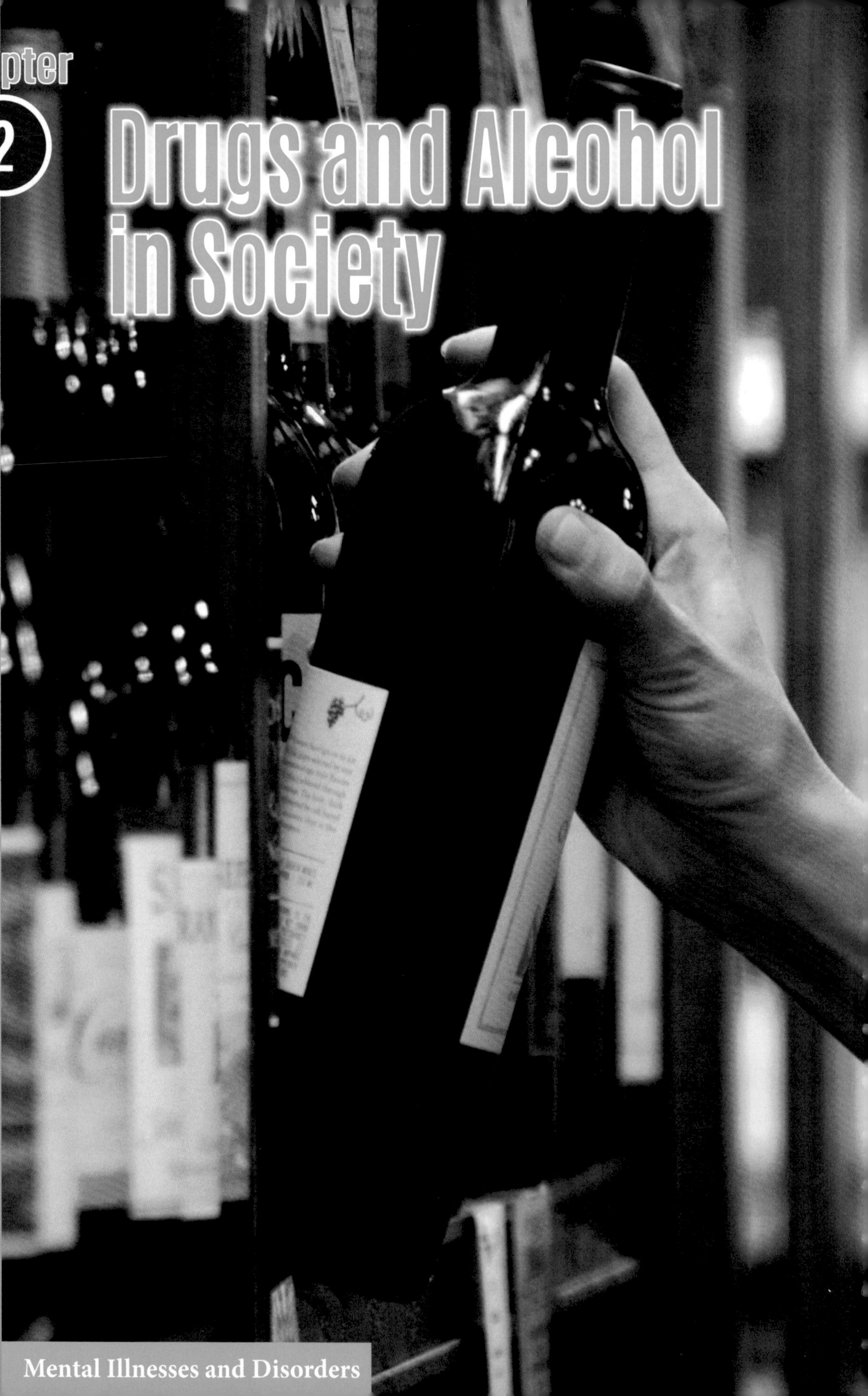

It is not certain when people first started using drugs. It is possible that it happened by accident. When early humans were searching for plants to eat, they may have discovered a substance with the power to affect the brain. Once the discovery was made, it is likely that some people continued using the substance to achieve the effect.

A Brief History of Drugs and Alcohol

Beverages, such as wine and beer, have been a part of the human experience for as long as there have been humans. For example, archaeologists have found jugs that probably held an early form of beer in the Neolithic period, dating from about 10,000 BC. Drinks made through **fermentation** soon became a key part of many religious rituals. People living on the island of Cyprus dissolved **opium** in both wine and water. Cyprus also exported opium to Egypt as early as 1500 BC. Drugs have not only been used for a very long time, they have also been part of the economy for nearly as long.

Ancient Egyptian tomb paintings dating from about 1500 BC depict people treading grapes to make wine.

In 2014, **60.9** million Americans admitted to **binge drinking.**

About **28** million Americans drive while intoxicated every year.

More than **16 million** Americans have admitted to heavy alcohol use.

During the American Civil War, morphine was used not only to treat pain but also to treat severe diarrhea, pneumonia, and bronchitis. Doctors treated patients with many addictive drugs that are illegal today.

War and Opium

Where there is trade, there is also conflict. For example, substance-related abuse helped cause the Opium War between China and Great Britain (1839–1842). Great Britain had brought opium into China, where it was traded for other goods. The result was widespread addiction among the Chinese people. During the war, China unsuccessfully tried to stop the importation of opium into the country.

Ingredients were extracted from opium and prescribed by physicians in the treatment of a wide variety of illnesses. Substances such as morphine and cocaine were legal and readily available. Many soldiers returned home from the American Civil War addicted to morphine, which had been given to them for pain caused by wounds. Ironically, when heroin was first produced, in 1874, it was thought that this drug would provide a cure for morphine addiction. As substance-related disorders became prevalent and some individuals died because of them, people began to recognize the dangers of drug addiction.

In the latter part of the nineteenth century and the early twentieth century, countries began to pass laws to control mind-altering substances. This is why, even today, people must be a particular age to drink alcohol or to buy cigarettes. Drugs and alcohol can have extreme effects on young bodies that are still developing. Laws try to prevent young people from taking drugs that could hurt their mental and physical development.

Drugs and Alcohol Today

There are so many possible bad effects of drugs, life might be easier if people just never took them at all. When it comes to cigarettes or illegal street drugs, that is definitely true. Some people feel that their lives are much better when they **abstain** from drugs and alcohol completely. People who are Buddhist avoid alcohol, while those who practice the Mormon faith avoid not only alcohol but also caffeine. Christian Scientists tend to avoid taking any medication.

Police use small, hand-held breath-testing devices to determine the level of alcohol in a driver's bloodstream.

A Deadly Combination

A popular trend among younger people is to switch between alcoholic drinks and energy drinks, or even to combine the two into one. Many brands of malt liquor, for example, have a high-caffeine content, and this is usually not reported on the label. Caffeine counteracts the depressant effect of the alcohol. On its own, alcohol will eventually make a person sleepy. When caffeine is added, that is less likely to happen.

People like this effect because they can party longer without getting tired. This is a very dangerous game. Combining the two drugs means that people do not realize just how much alcohol they have consumed. This makes both alcohol poisoning and alcohol-related injuries much more likely.

Plenty of other people decide to abstain from alcohol for personal reasons that have nothing to do with religion. They might not care for the taste of it, for example, or they might have had a family member who struggled with addiction.

The Beneficial Effects

Some people think that there are many instances where drugs are not harmful and are even beneficial. For example, people suffering from chronic pain need to take drugs regularly in order to live their lives. Doctors have found that in small quantities, drinking wine or coffee can actually provide health benefits. Studies have suggested that moderate amounts of wine can be good for the human heart, while caffeine consumption may have an association with lower rates of dementia and certain cancers.

Some doctors think that a substance in red wine called resveratrol may help prevent coronary artery disease, which is the condition that leads to heart attacks.

If people choose to include these substances in their lives, there are certain things to remember so they can embrace the good effects while limiting the bad ones.

Practice Moderation Legal drugs such as caffeine and alcohol can usually be used in small amounts without doing any real harm. Bingeing is not good for any part of the body.

Avoid Other People's Drugs Every bottle of prescription drugs has a name printed on the label. If that name is someone else's, put the bottle down.

There Are Reasons for Laws Certain drugs are illegal because they can easily destroy someone's life. Alcohol, on the other hand, is legal for adults but not for children because it is not safe for younger people. It is important to remember that these rules are not designed to stop people having enjoyment in life. These laws exist to help keep people safe.

However, even when people try to practice moderation and follow the rules, the truth is that some people, both adults and children, can develop problems with drugs and alcohol These problems occur when people become **dependent** on the substance they are taking. Their dependence starts to affect their quality of life, health, and relationships.

SUBSTANCE-RELATED DISORDERS

The *Diagnostic and Statistical Manual of Mental Disorders* (*DSM*) lists 11 criteria that doctors use to diagnose a substance-related disorder. The criteria are divided into four groups.

IMPAIRED CONTROL

These criteria relate to the difficulty someone has in stopping use of the drug.

1. The person takes larger amounts than intended, or takes the substance for a longer period than intended.

2. The person attempts to "cut back" but cannot.

3. The person devotes large amounts of time to getting, using, and recovering from the drug.

4. The person feels regular cravings for the drug.

SOCIAL IMPAIRMENT

These criteria relate to the negative impact of the drug on the person's life.

5. Drug use interferes with duties at work or school.

6. Drug use causes problems with friends, family members, or coworkers.

7. The person gives up other activities in favor of using the drug.

RISKY USE

These criteria relate to the person's use of the drug even when it is likely to cause harm.

8. The person uses the drug in situations that are physically dangerous.

9. The person continues using the drug even though he or she knows that it causes physical or emotional problems.

PHARMACOLOGICAL CRITERIA

These relate to the chemical impact of the drug on the body.

10. The person has an increased tolerance for the drug, meaning that it takes more to achieve the same effect.

11. The person experiences **withdrawal** symptoms when the drug is not used.

What Is Dependence?

Human beings depend on eating, drinking, and breathing to stay alive. Some people also depend on particular medicines to stay healthy. For example, people with diabetes need to carefully monitor a substance called insulin. If their insulin levels get too low, they must inject some more so that they do not get sick.

A lot of adults feel like they "depend" on their morning coffee. They have trouble waking up in the morning if they do not get that jolt of caffeine. While it is not great to be dependent on caffeine, doctors do not usually worry about it too much. Most people can usually break the coffee habit without too much trouble. Avoiding caffeine will probably cause the person to have some headaches at first. The pain is caused by the body craving the caffeine but not getting it. Doctors call this a withdrawal symptom. In a few days or so, the body will adjust to living without caffeine, and the headaches will go away.

There are a small number of people who get severe caffeine addictions, and they may need the help of a doctor to stop.

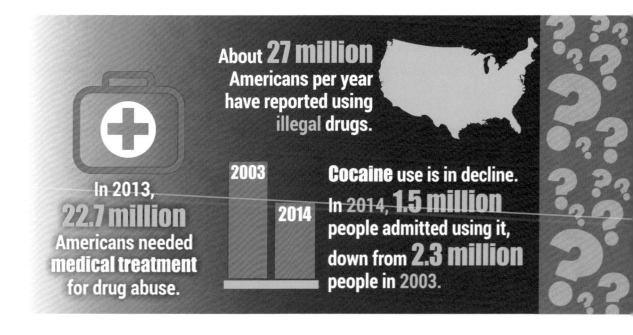

About **27 million** Americans per year have reported using illegal drugs.

In 2013, **22.7 million** Americans needed **medical treatment** for drug abuse.

2003

2014

Cocaine use is in decline. In 2014, **1.5 million** people admitted using it, down from **2.3 million** people in 2003.

Other forms of dependence are more troubling. For example, people often talk about how hard it is to quit smoking. There are mental and physical reasons for this. First, smoking becomes a habit that people simply get used to doing, and this is the mental part of the dependency. Second, the body gets used to having nicotine regularly. When the nicotine is taken away, the withdrawal symptoms can be rough. People can feel bad tempered and even ill. Doctors all agree that it is well worth suffering through the withdrawal in order to quit smoking. Anyone who has quit will say it is very difficult to do, though.

People who have given up nicotine can suffer withdrawal symptoms such as a cough, headaches, and flu symptoms.

Substance-Related Disorders

It can be hard for others to understand why people would keep smoking even when they know it is bad for their health. This is how an addiction works. People who are addicted to something keep on using or doing that thing even when they know they should not They often feel like they *have* to continue even when they do not *want* to do it anymore. If people become so dependent on a drug that they keep taking it even though it hurts them, doctors describe that condition as a substance-use disorder.

Addiction or Disorder?

Many people use the terms "drug addiction" and "drug addict" to describe dependency on a substance. Most doctors, though, prefer to avoid using the word "addiction." Although it is very commonly used in regular speech, the word "addiction" is too vague as a diagnosis. "Substance-use disorder" is the preferred term because it is more specific and sounds less negative.

A substance-use disorder involves serious and negative consequences from regular use of a substance over a 12-month period. When a person has this disorder, he or she continues to use the substance even though many problems occur as a result.

For example, a teenager who is dependent on alcohol might vomit, have terrible headaches, and generally feel sick from drinking the night before. She might skip class because she feels sick, or hungover, or she might do so to spend more time drinking. She might steal money to buy alcohol. She might go to parties with people she does not know well who could hurt her. She might drive while drunk or get in a car with someone else who is drunk. These are all negative consequences, but someone with a substance-use disorder will continue using the drug anyway.

A second type of drug and alcohol problem is called substance-**induced** disorder. This term refers to problems beyond the actual addiction. Substance-induced disorders include the physical or mental problems that can be caused by usage of the drug, such the withdrawal symptoms. Sometimes these two types of disorder, substance-use and substance-induced, are simply collected together and called substance-related disorders.

Some people become dependent on substances such as nicotine and alcohol, while others do not. Doctors think that genetics and a person's environment are important factors in substance-use disorders.

Symptoms

Symptoms of drug and alcohol disorders vary a lot, depending on the substance being used. They are also determined by the person's body chemistry, the amount of substance used, the duration of use, and other factors. The most common symptoms include poor thinking, judgment, **perception**, and attention. The person who has the substance-use disorder may have difficulty staying awake.

Alternatively, he might have so much energy that he is awake and active all night. The way someone acts toward others will often be far different than it would be if the substance were not being used.

When used **recreationally**, as opposed to use for medical reasons, drugs create a state of **intoxication**. As a result, people say and do things while using drugs and alcohol that they would not normally say or do. It is common for people with this disorder to feel shame as a result. It is also common for people to not even remember what happened while they were intoxicated. This is called a "blackout," and it is usually a sign of a serious dependence problem.

Repeated drug and alcohol use in teenagers can present some serious health and social risks, including loss of interest in regular activities and failing at school.

Why Is Dependence a Problem?

When a person uses a drug, it interferes with the brain's natural chemical activities. If the drug is used regularly, the brain gets used to the addictive substances and begins to "expect" them. This is why someone who normally drinks coffee every day might get a headache if she tries to skip a day. Over time, tolerance builds up, and the coffee drinker might need two cups of coffee to feel the effect she used to get from one.

What Is Tolerance?

Most people who abuse a drug will develop tolerance to the chemical effects on the body. This means that they have to take more to get the effect they want. Some people brag that they can "hold their liquor." In other words, they are proud of their ability to drink so much without acting drunk. They do not realize, though, that this is actually a symptom of alcohol abuse.

It is important to understand that all drugs, even medicine given by doctors, can be dangerous if used incorrectly. Depending on the drug, vital organs such as the liver and kidneys can be injured. In some cases, such as with alcohol or cigarettes, the likelihood of developing cancer or heart disease will increase.

As tolerance builds, it takes more of the drug for the person to feel the effects. The person increases the amount of the drug used. This, in turn, increases the negative impacts on the body. Meanwhile, the negative impacts on the person's life will also increase. If she tries to stop using the drug, she may find she is unable to do so. In fact, it can be dangerous for someone with a severe drug dependence to stop suddenly. Quitting after the brain has built up tolerance to a substance causes even more chemical disruption in the brain. This is why people with substance-induced disorders usually need some form of medical help to quit.

Misuse of prescription drugs such as painkillers can damage vital body organs or even cause death.

Take a deeper look

Do some research on the negative effects of alcohol use on health. Cover topics such as how much do doctors think is okay, what health problems can result from excess drinking, and how can an adult tell what is too much drinking and what is a moderate amount. Write a short paragraph on each of these topics.

Treating Drug and Alcohol Dependence

It is not easy, but with effort, people can recover from substance-related disorders. Withdrawal symptoms are often extremely unpleasant, and until fairly recently, people with substance-related disorders were expected to conquer them "cold turkey." This expression means stopping the use of a substance and then suffering through whatever happens next. Fortunately, treatment facilities now exist where people with substance-related disorders can get professional help for their problems. The most successful treatments often combine the use of medication with therapy.

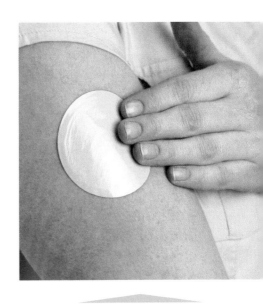

Some people find it easier to quit smoking with nicotine patches. These deliver a measured dose of nicotine to ease the withdrawal symptoms.

Medication

Scientists developed medications that can help to reduce the symptoms of withdrawal. Medications have also been developed to help individuals avoid **relapse**. Substance-related disorders are complex, though, and while medicine can be helpful in treatment, it is usually not enough to break the pattern of substance addiction. People have a better chance at recovery if medications are combined with counseling or participation in a recovery program.

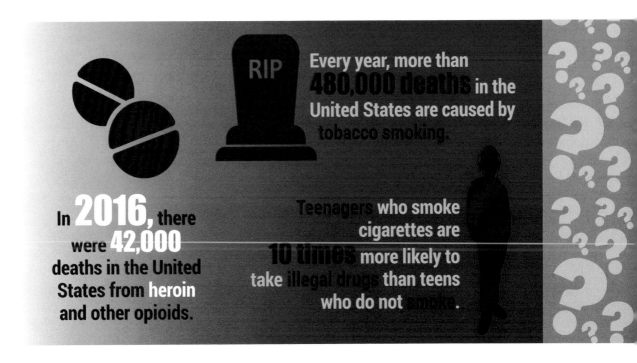

RIP

Every year, more than **480,000 deaths** in the United States are caused by tobacco smoking.

In **2016**, there were **42,000** deaths in the United States from **heroin and other opioids**.

Teenagers who smoke cigarettes are **10 times** more likely to take **illegal drugs** than teens who do not **smoke**.

Social gatherings often involve alcohol, which can be difficult for people working to overcome a substance-related disorder. It is possible to have fun without drinking, though.

Therapy

Everything people see and do, including talking, has the power to affect their brain. Talking to a therapist or members of a self-help group can be a very powerful form of treatment for a substance-related disorder. **Cognitive** behavioral therapy (CBT) involves training in social and coping skills and is among the most successful treatments.

The goal in CBT is for the person to be better able to express herself and to interact appropriately in various situations. These skills can reduce a person's daily anxieties and struggles and may make it easier for her to avoid the temptation to use drugs. CBT also involves looking at the thoughts, or "triggers," that cause drug use and teaches patients ways to change or avoid these triggers.

Sometimes, CBT is used with a technique called motivational interviewing. This helps people to identify the pros and cons of changing their behavior in order to help them make needed changes. Family therapy is also useful in dealing with substance-related disorders. It helps a family know how to help the individual in crisis and how to keep the family unit healthy and together.

Other Treatments

Many people with anxiety or depression find relief through meditation and relaxation techniques. These same techniques have also helped people with substance problems. Breathing deeply helps to clear the mind of all thoughts and to calm and relax the body. With meditation, a person allows thoughts to float through the mind, while remaining detached. Gentle stretching, deep breathing, and mind-soothing exercises such as those found in yoga can be very helpful in reducing the depression that often comes with having a substance-related disorder.

Some people find meditation very helpful in dealing with substance-related disorders.

Some people report that **acupuncture** has helped to reduce their cravings for specific substances. It has been used successfully to treat cravings in individuals addicted to cocaine and nicotine. Alternative remedies for substance abuse disorders may also include herbs, vitamins, and dietary supplements, some of which have been used for centuries by peoples around the world. However, herbs, vitamins, and dietary supplements are not regulated by the government in the way that traditional medicines are.

Take a deeper look

Find out more about what resources are available in your area. Does your school have a Drug Abuse Resistance Education (DARE) program? If so, what services does it offer? You might search online for 2-1-1, a program run by United Way, which collects information about local resources for dealing with substance-related disorders. Also check to see what groups, such as Alateen, meet in your area. Write a short paper that lists the different services available.

AA groups follow the 12 traditions, in addition to the 12 steps. One of these traditions is that it is the primary purpose of each group to carry its message to the alcoholic who still suffers.

The 12 Steps

The best-known treatment for substance abuse in North America is Alcoholics Anonymous (AA). AA does not advocate the use of any psychiatric medications as part of treatment. Instead, it relies on attending regular group meetings and following a 12-step program. AA is a self-directed program, and people follow the steps at their own pace. Members of the group share their own experiences.

AA has changed the lives of many people, but it is not the answer for everyone. Some people, for example, have a hard time with the religious component of AA. People who are not religious may find that aspect uncomfortable or inappropriate. There are increasing numbers of humanist or agnostic AA meetings, which follow the same basic rules but do not put as much emphasis on religion.

Many other 12-step programs have been modeled after AA. These include Narcotics Anonymous and Cocaine Anonymous. Al-Anon and Alateen are groups for the families of people with alcohol dependency.

Living with Drug and Alcohol Dependence

I t can be hard to cope when a family member or close friend has a substance-related disorder. There are some strategies that can improve the quality of life for people with the disorder and their loved ones.

Be Understanding

This is a painful type of disorder to have, and the social **stigma** can be difficult to deal with. Try to be understanding.

Admit the Problem

Admitting that there is a problem, to oneself, to a friend, or to a counselor, is the first step toward recovery.

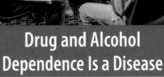

Get Help

Even if a person will not accept help, there are groups with resources to help friends and family members, such as Alateen.

It Is Nobody's Fault

No one is to blame. People do not drink too much or misuse drugs because of weakness or what someone else does.

Drug and Alcohol Dependence Is a Disease

A person with a drug or alcohol dependence has a disease, and the problem can be treated. People recover every day.

Community Resources

Talk to others with similar problems. Many communities have local centers that offer help for substance-related disorders.

Drug and Alcohol Dependence over Time

Substances that intoxicate and relax people have been in use for thousands of years, perhaps even tens of thousands of years. Just as they have positive effects, though, they can have negative consequences, too. Drug and alcohol abuse is part of human history.

375 BC

The ancient Greek playwright Eubulus described how people who drank more than the accepted three bowls of alcohol became violent after the fourth bowl, and then their behavior got steadily worse until, by the tenth bowl, they would throw furniture.

1574 AD

A Venetian visitor to Constantinople, which today is Istanbul in Turkey, reported how people became addicted to an opium drink. A century later, people in China began mixing opium with tobacco and smoking it in pipes, which led to widespread dependence.

1895

Heroin, produced from opium, was marketed in Germany. It was hoped it may be less addictive than morphine as a drug. During the Civil War, many wounded soldiers became addicted to morphine that was given as a painkiller.

Until recently, treatment for substance-related disorders centered on the individual. Today, doctors advise all family members to get the help and support they need.

1919

The manufacture and sale of "intoxicating liquors" was prohibited in the United States after strong lobbying from the **temperance** movement. Prohibition led to widespread corruption and lawlessness and was repealed in 1931.

1935

Alcoholics Anonymous was set up in Akron, Ohio. Its early members devised a 12-step system to help people who are alcoholics. Today, there are estimated to be more than 2 million members of AA all over the world, with 1.3 million members in the United States.

2016

On World No Tobacco Day, on May 31, the World Health Organization (WHO) called on governments around the world to prepare for plain packaging of tobacco products. Australia was the first country to introduce plain packaging, in 2012.

Quiz

1 What is the age group most at risk from inhaling drugs?

2 What is tolerance to a drug?

3 About how many liters of alcohol a year does the average person drink in the United States?

4 How many preventable deaths is alcohol responsible for each year in the United States?

5 What is the main source of nicotine?

6 Where did Great Britain fight a war in order to force the local people to buy drugs?

7 What causes withdrawal symptoms?

8 What are substance-induced disorders?

9 What are the two deadly diseases caused by cigarette smoking?

10 What does the term "cold turkey" mean?

ANSWERS

1 People aged 12 to 15 **2** A person has to take more to get the effect he or she wants. **3** About 9 **4** About 88,000 **5** Tobacco plants **6** China **7** The body is craving the drug and reacts in a painful way. **8** Disorders caused by the use of a drug, such as poor thinking and perception **9** Cancer and heart disease **10** Stopping the use of a drug and then suffering the painful consequences for the body

Key Words

abstain: to choose not to take part in a particular activity

acupuncture: an ancient Chinese treatment that involves pricking the body with needles at specific points

addiction: a strong physical or mental need for a particular substance or activity

asphyxiation: when oxygen is cut off

cognitive: having to do with the thought process

dependent: needing something a lot

depressants: substances that slow down bodily functions

fermentation: a chemical process that, for example, turns grapes into wine

hypnotics: types of drugs that cause sleep

induced: brought on

intoxication: an excited state in which a person is not in control of his of her actions

moderation: limited in amount, not extreme

opioids: substances resembling opium in their effects

opium: an addictive drug made from the opium poppy

perception: awareness or understanding of something

psychological: relating to the human mind and behavior

recreationally: done for fun, or with no specific reason

relapse: getting worse after a period of getting better, when someone who had stopped using drugs starts using again

sedatives: substances that make a person calm or sleepy

seizures: sudden, involuntary physical reactions, sometimes caused by a chemical imbalance in the body

stigma: negative ideas or feelings about something

stimulant: a substance that speeds up bodily functions

temperance: abstaining from alcoholic drink

withdrawal: taking something away

Index

Log on to www.av2books.com

AV² by Weigl brings you media enhanced books that support active learning. Go to www.av2books.com, and enter the special code found on page 2 of this book. You will gain access to enriched and enhanced content that supplements and complements this book. Content includes video, audio, weblinks, quizzes, a slide show, and activities.

AV² Online Navigation

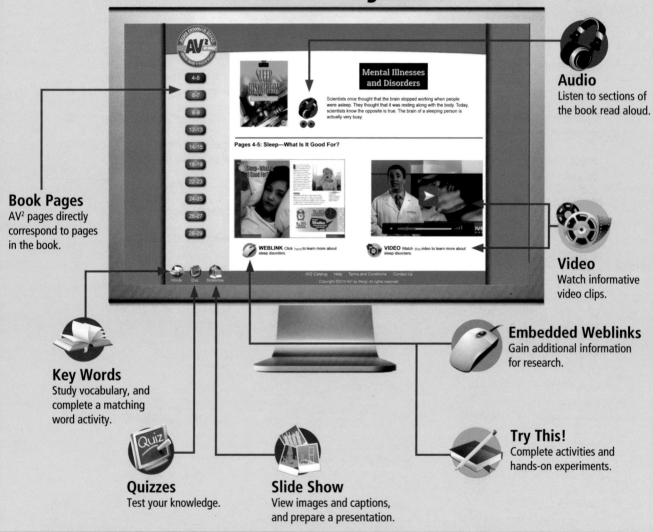

Audio
Listen to sections of the book read aloud.

Book Pages
AV² pages directly correspond to pages in the book.

Video
Watch informative video clips.

Key Words
Study vocabulary, and complete a matching word activity.

Embedded Weblinks
Gain additional information for research.

Try This!
Complete activities and hands-on experiments.

Quizzes
Test your knowledge.

Slide Show
View images and captions, and prepare a presentation.

AV² was built to bridge the gap between print and digital. We encourage you to tell us what you like and what you want to see in the future.

Sign up to be an AV² Ambassador at www.av2books.com/ambassador.